THOUGHTS ON LIFE

IN RHYME & SCULPTURE

END OF AN ERA

DENNIS GRAY

ASPIRE
PUBLISHING HUB LLC.

Thoughts on Life in Rhyme & Sculpture

ISBN
978-1-960758-03-3 (Paperback)
978-1-960758-04-0 (eBook)
978-1-960758-05-7 (Hardcover)

THOUGHTS ON LIFE

IN RHYME & SCULPTURE

Table of Contents

Part I – The Meaning of Life

PART II – PURSUING THE PURPOSE

PART III – THE WONDERS, THE BUMMERS

Part IV – End Of An Era

Part V – Thoughts Captured In Sculpture

A Balancing Act

Children on a teeter-totter sensing vulnerability,
Skiers on an icy slope testing their agility,
Performers juggling balls or blocks, a firebaton or knife,
Each aware of how they dare
The balancing act of life.

Riders at full gallop in extreme exhilaration,
Accountants, students, shoppers playing numbers allocation,
President, captain, secretary, grandparent, husband, wife—
Each also aware how precarious
Is the balancing act of life.

Upon awakening daily, that balancing act is on.
By the time the picture sharpens, precious moments quickly gone.
Conflicts are immediate: work or play? Fight or flee?
Eat or drink? Pain or pleasure?
Them or us or you or me?

Balancing luxury with necessity, selflessness with greed,
The moment versus the morrow; does one follow, stall, or lead?
While the spokes around all provocate with risk of stress and strife,
Still most do dare, with little care,
The balancing act of life.

At work, it's competence that must balance politics;
At home, it's about attention paid to spouse and pets and kids;
With relatives, the financial stuff always seems so imminent;
With friends and most acquaintances,
It's just about time commitment.

Balancing a canoe or bike, the first step of a tot,
Give an absolute sense of right or wrong; one either succeeds or not.
Hardly like juggling life's options, without pattern or design,
While expected to justly allocate
Priorities and time.

Any expectation of doing so, for better or for worse,
Without "offending" someone, is ridiculously perverse.
Just as the scales of justice teeter-totter in a breeze,
Our perspective for decision
Is a matter of degrees.

Life's no more than a balancing act, with each of us on stage.
No rights or wrongs, ifs, ands, or buts; we react and turn the page.
Visioning a juggler on a high-wire, with the balance he contrives,
May be the clearest picture.
Of the balance in our lives.

On Perspective

Perspective is the key to life—to coping with it all.
To comprehending why we're here, existing on this ball
of dirt and rock and water, of people, plants, and bugs.
We fight to keep our balance against the pulls and tugs
of oft-competing voices, with oft-conflicting thought.
It's hard to even hear them all—much less grasp what we ought!
Yet the search for one's perspective on what their purpose *is*
can, in itself, become a tail that wags the dog. Who says
that any more exists in life than getting through each day?
Or witnessing the rise and set of our sun's incredulous rays?

Some think there should be more to life—perhaps it is religion,
or servitude, or sex exploits, or even narcissism.
Or maybe just the simple recognition that each day
the sun goes up and down again, and never does it sway.
Perhaps the fact that we perceive days differing from another
is just a figment in our mind, while moments parody each other.
Perspective is the way we look at any given scene,
or a glass half full or empty, and interpret what it means.
Perspective is the answer for concern with what one "sees"
since, with slightly different focus, the picture changes with ease.

We humans spend a lot of time concerned what something means,
when reality could be nothing more than "it *is* just as it seems."
We seldom recognize the fact that in the search for "why?"
we lose the forest for the trees—we seldom even try
to experience a day's events as just *what* life's about.

(The aberration, here and there, is a daily routine throughout.)
And if we stop to do that—to end the constant quest
for "why" and "how" and "would" and "should," "which god" and all the rest—
then it's just maybe possible that we could feel a sense
of being *in* the moment, being *in* the present tense.

Experiencing life for what it is, one moment at a time,
allows us to glimpse the Master's plan—nature so sublime!
The sight, the smell, the taste, the touch, without evaluation,
are maybe just the point of life—the purpose of creation.
Alas, if true, another thought: What source provides direction?
"Am I a cause, or just effect?" becomes a probing question.
Is it any wonder we're a confused and worried lot,
since decades of attention to analysis and thought
have left our searching souls in a sorry, sorry state—
still lost without the answers or a map to heaven's gate?

Perspective is an attitude that changes over time;
whether one's expands or shrinks depends on frame of mind.
Some learn to just experience without judging wrong or right.
Others turn a cheek to those who trespassed in the night.
But many fail to get that far. As strange as it may seem,
lives remain a string of episodes without a conscious stream.
They learn from some but run from most, so often feel confused.
They laugh and cry and sing or shout, bewildered and abused,
and still expend their energy with every rising sun,
expecting answers to their questions, which "any day will come..."

Perspective is indeed the key to coping with it all
amidst the billion sights and sounds and tastes and scents that call
for instant grasp and prompt response, each moment of the day.
Consistency or chaos—nerve-wracking either way.
Perspective requires pause and thought when no answer is in sight,
not painting a picture black or bleak—but experiencing it as bright.
The beauty and the splendor are the pleasure of the "now."
Perspective helps prolong the wonder; don't bother wondering how.
We need to learn to appreciate the moment that we're in
and experience it as the gift of life; to fail to is a sin.

Waste of Time

Often now I ponder how, ignoring common sense,
we allow ourselves, with nonchalance, to so readily accept
imprisonment to a system of unintelligible direction
which so overwhelmingly controls, irrespective of intention,

our most perishable commodity, most rare and precious gift,
most important of life's treasures? Are we, the species, daft-
accepting evident destiny which steals our asset blind?
How dare we say that it's okay to allow the waste of time?

Ignoring personal agenda for how or which or where,
the factor which controls is "*when*" one gets from here to there.
A freeway trip, a checkout line, an airline terminal gate,
now the 11th Commandment: "just hurry up and wait."

Race, religion, wealth or power, being smarter or nicer,
are irrelevant facts at a traffic light - the world's great equalizer.
Living within our system demands ultimate sacrifice;
we exhaust the sole commodity irreplaceable at any price.

"Could the system change for better?" is the dilemma which we face.
To conserve more precious moments and avoid the ludicrous waste
of minutes, hours, days and weeks waiting patiently in line?
Ultimately waiting for *godot?* What incredible waste of time.

Some claim life's full of shortcuts, any means justified by the end.
Some think just butting in is fair, since rules are meant to bend.
Others find the answer by consuming time in haste;
despite attendant stress & strain, loath to let time waste.

We're told the universe expands, ever increasing in its speed.
We're told time, too, accelerates - "time flies" our daily creed.
So with less and less available, and more and more expended,
how can we, with such simplicity, treat time as open-ended?

Should not we be a bit concerned that imploding in our lap
is the very raison d'étre: the time to just relax,
to witness the world's wonders and beauty of life sublime?
What a crime, so many waste this precious gift of time.

On Conflict; Life's Simple Patterns

Most conflict stems from hesitance to change of any kind,
since people are most comfortable with stability over time.
Expansion, Innovation, Growth —concepts clearly all-in fashion—
involving commitment to personal change, seldom made with passion.
We forget about life's simple patterns, as our time is scarcely rationed.

In a world of random circumstances, overwhelming on most days,
It's hard to keep a vision of how the Big Picture overlays.
With complexity and chaos so evident all around,
as conflict and uncertainty then naturally abound,
we forget that life's simple patterns are of symbol, sight and sound.

While people march to different beats, nature's rhythm is everywhere.
Whispering wind, crashing waves, birds soaring on air.
Conflict comes from man-made noise, from engines, horns and shouts
competing with commercials, creating hesitancy and self-doubts,
while we forget about life's simple patterns—what life is all about.

Conflict also often stems from what we think we see
    when hesitant to take a deeper look at alternative reality.
Compare the spectrum of a rainbow or magnificent open sky
    with gawky buildings or billboards, whose architects somehow deny
that life's patterns favor continuity of beauty over time.

With society having largely become a giant gambling game,
    whether stocks or homes or lotteries, the conflict is the same.
Caused by competition of people pursuing personal worth,
    'survival of the fittest' somehow become our creed from birth,
while the simplest rhythmic patterns control our time on earth.

ON INTIMACY

True intimacy is rare, an experience too many miss,
when feelings of togetherness, connectedness, and bliss
unite to know the wondrous pleasure and purity
of purposeful relationship—that feeling: *meant to be.*

Still rarer are the moments when the element of passion
further intensifies feelings of closeness and connection.
Intensity not from anger or jealousy or lust,
but from fusing heart and mind with unconditional trust

that the person you're connected to is worthy of your love,
that attitudes and expectations fit like hand and glove,
then recognize such rarity, with ability to appreciate
the fortune of having found a genuine soul mate.

With touch, taste, vision, scent, and hearing all in sync,
with intimacy evolving from your mind and body link,
flows enchantment, contentment, and magic combined
to let wonder and purpose of life intertwine.

Too seldom are those moments when connection and intensity
with passion combine to allow true intimacy.

ON INSPIRATION

From the world around us creativity springs,
sparking imagination to take wings.
From dreams or visions, from joy or frustration,
any spark can lead to true Inspiration.

Artist, writer, composer, musician,
architect, engineer, dancer, magician-
those who pursue challenge of creation
well know the value of true Inspiration.

Aroused by senses of taste or smell,
of seeing or hearing or touch, as well
as ESP (the extra sensory perception),
any spark can lead to a suggestion

which feeds human spirit from art to fashion,
fueling creativity, excitement and passion.
In a chaotic world, with vision often bleak,
Inspiration is a value that all should seek.

On Tranquility

The whisper of tranquility is present in the now,
    with wonder there for us to grasp, if we would but allow
ourselves to sense the splendor which truly tranquil moments bring—
    the awareness and acceptance that such moments are the dream.

In flicker of a candle or the eyelash of a child,
    from quivering leaves in a gentle breeze or a lover's loving smile,
in the silent twinkling of a star, a softly soaring bird,
    or a smoothly sailing group of clouds which float without a word.

It's those seconds of serenity which, for taking, could be ours—
    but are mostly missed while we focus on the minutes and the hours
in our race against the hands of time, presuming that our goal,
    while looking past the obvious in the search to find our soul.

Some search a path forever thru study and education;
    others pursue poetry or prayer or meditation.
In many walks of life, we find that effort breeds success.
    One can achieve an end result thru commitment and practice.

But finding true tranquility takes nothing of the sort;
    it simply takes a willingness to develop a rapport
with the truly marvelous instances which happen all the time
    in every phase of nature's way. True wonder is sublime.

The whisper of tranquility is there for us to grasp.
    Without a clearer goal in sight, life's purpose is, perhaps,
to simply, with awareness and acceptance, fully sense
    the wonder of such moments — tranquility in our presence.

In The Depths Of A Dream

In the darkness of sleep, as magic takes hold,
the vapor of vision begins—
encouraged by spirits of moments and memories
replaying past scenes, songs and sins
which may or not have transpired, in fact,
in the timeframe which most call reality.
But as visions unfold in the depths of your dreams,
one approaches the boundaries of sanity.

From the depth of sleep you can gently escape
to a state of unparalleled bliss,
where unlimited vision of an infinite landscape
draws a picture with nothing amiss.
At a point, you'll detach from the fuzzy collage
to step up and away from the scene,
where the view to behold is beholden to none—
a perspective unique to a dream.

From the chamber of sleep, soon a soft haze of color
    forms a rainbow-rimmed tunnel to glimpse
your potential connection to life's deepest question:
    What's the point of it all? What's the sense?
From perspective above the strange vision below,
    at the awesome threshold of dream,
you'll see faces familiar, others marked with intention—
    some concerned, some absurd, some obscene.

In the shadows of sleep, creep the shadows of torment,
    of evil, of fear, even rage;
a fantasy performance in kaleidoscope set
    —perhaps just alter ego on stage?
But your choice is distinct, from this vantage on high,
    to confront your true nature, or hide
from the spirits of moments and memories called forth.
    It's in sleep's depth, you're truly alive.

The Spectrum Of Passion

Our balance in life goes out of control
when instinctive pursuit of passion
consumes time and energy to a level
which evolves into obsession.

Passion - likely the most powerful influence
in behavior, motivation and drive –
inspires creations of music, art, writings,
pursuers of science and purpose of life.

The driving force in sexual connections,
the critical element of feeling 'in love,'
prompter of anger, resentment and evil –
passion's power and dark side equally strong.

Thieves, killers, perverts, criminals of all kind,
provoked by passion beyond human laws,
religious zealots obsessed with hate—
passionately willing to die for their 'cause.'

Others develop a passion for risk
which results in obsession to gamble,
pre-empting every other priority
to roll dice, flip cards, or yank a slot handle.

Obsessive pursuits in passionate people
    too often generate demands so extreme
that passion keeps pushing above and beyond
    any possible point of retreat.

In some, passion develops to sheer selfish greed –
    intoxication for money, power, control,
stock market profits, 'winning' the game
    at any cost, to meet some higher goal.

Passion plays havoc with energy,
    ranging from exhilaration to despair,
from moments of blissful intimacy
    to loneliness beyond compare.

Still, balancing the dark side
    which always results from obsessive dimension,
how incomplete our lives would be,
    without the wonder and beauty of passion.

Useless Aggravation

Is it a lazy person who just 'accepts' a situation?
Is it a wimpy person who bypasses confrontation?
Or is it simple wisdom to avoid useless aggravation?
Is patience a virtue which many know?
Or do they get frustrated when something moves slow?
Would a wiser course of action be to just let it go?
I think so.

The Soft Voice Of Spring Rain

Tiny toes dancing on a plastic mat,
Static in the airwaves, that quiet crickly crack,
Gentle tap tapping on the skylite of a shack-
Hear the soft voice of spring rain.

Peaceful streams of water swirl through muddy holes
Exerting calming influence on seas of transient souls,
Nourishing plants & animals, supporting nature's goals –
Thank the soft voice of spring rain.

Gathering momentum on the downward course it takes,
Headed with deliberateness toward streams, rivers and lakes,
Then ultimately to the sea, with surging crashing breaks –
All the soft voice of spring rain.

Rippling waves fwack the shore with rhythm of a psalm ,-
As serenity emanates from breezy leaves of palm,
And stressfulness evaporates as breezes gently calm –
Once the soft voice of spring rain.

My mind at ease and body relaxed,
My senses heightened to the max,
Temporarily spared from life's attacks –
Bless the soft voice of spring rain.

LAST LOVE

'Love' comes and goes along the years, in varying degrees
of connection and commitment, of passion, wants and needs.
In childhood, feelings fluctuate on any given day,
as friends & family witness moodshifts of Love and Hate.
During adolescent years, Love struggles against teen Guilt;
then by high-school graduation, the balance turns full-tilt

as Love tends to become defined 'however necessary'
to provide justifiable rationale for romantic promiscuity.
Then come the yuppie worklife years, when egos strong yet fragile
finally begin to register that Love means something special.
First Loves are so important since they set one down a path.
Second Loves more relevant, perspective more relaxed.

Next Loves are likely spouses, seeming a good idea at the time,
though best intentions often fail to hold the marriage line.
Last Love is the important one,
the soul mate which most search,
a partner who's their complement,
who makes their life on earth
fulfilling, joyous, meaningful and each experience better.
Last Love is the point of life – the true raison d'etre.

PART II

PURSUING THE PURPOSE

About Focus

When your focus on existence becomes about the things you own
and pleasure of the moment gets pre-empted by a phone.
When you recognize your world of colors turning monotone,
do you ponder the unknown?

When pattern keeps repeating and becomes your life routine,
so everything seems yin or yang with nothing in between,
When you recognize the world around you having turned obscene,
are you following your dream?

When novels/art/music are pre-empted by remote control,
and the more you try to change your life, the deeper looks your hole,
When you sense the way you're headed doesn't lead to any goal,
do you wonder of your soul?

When your focus of attention is immediate in need
and the cause of present tension stems from pursuing greed.
When you recognize selfishness as the priority you heed,
is it time to intercede?

When your focus on the HERE and NOW is all that you envision
    versus WHERE you wish to get to and how every next decision
almost certainly impacts your eventual position,
    is your path toward any mission?

Reality is just a collective hunch--not black or white, but gray.
    It's time to get a focus where you wish to be some day,
or a time will come when you may find it impossible to say
    if you've ever found your way.

Eyes Focused Upside Down

In a world so near the precipice of catastrophic war,
as peoples' trust in leadership has crashed along some shore,
and confidence in the Future has been shaken to the core…
So many just wait hopelessly, with eyes focused on the floor.

Absence of security has become accepted norm,
as people on congested streets see fear in every form,
watching quietly as culture evolves from Classics to street porn…
Weary people staring down, looking so forlorn.

Led by politicians who believe themselves apart
from natural laws which dictate that voting from the heart,
instead of mindful logic, is really not so smart…
While deadened eyes look down – unlikely to restart.

In a world of oxymorons where 'young adults' abound,
'awfully good' at 'doing nothing' – awaiting 'future' to be found,
always pending 'opinions' to spread 'constant change' around…
But eyes stay focused on the floor, lost in 'silent sound.'

In theory, we're the species with presence of mind and thought
to respond to craziness as this with counter-steps, which ought
to arrest the trends of hopelessness, before it's all for naught...
Yet eyes stay focused downward, ignoring what's been taught.

Instead dreaming of tropical islands enthralling with delight,
enchanting, enlightening, empowering our psyche,
avoiding concerns or problems by pushing out of sight...
Eyes stay down, not focused on matters of wrong or right.

In a world so near the precipice of catastrophic war,
as peoples' trust in leadership has crashed along some shore,
and confidence in the Future has been shaken to the core...
So many just wait hopelessly, eyes focused on the floor.

The Moment

The here and now is where we're at; The Moment is the deal.
The why? or how? or if? or when? not relevant, not real.

When one confronts the issue of "The Purpose of it all,"
what more than any Moment could one sensibly recall
as being both the means and end to pleasure or to pain?
What more or less could one expect to accomplish or to gain?

The Moment passes hastily; so easy to miss
its beauty and wonder, its value and bliss.

And yet, we'll let The Moment all too often pass us by.
We'll sit and wait and watch and wince 'till its too late to try.
Observation? Yes, it's clear enough that all one ought to do,
is recognize and appreciate each Moment's splendid hue.

So why don't you?

Capacity To Care

How seldom one cares about anything else
than personal needs, desires, or self
(the product of culture, technology, wealth)
Leaving little capacity to care…

In a world with priority focus on Me,
irrespective of age or maturity,
with Pleasure the measure of reality,
No time left for capacity to care…

A baby's priorities are food, toys and swings;
third grade ballerinas become angels with wings;
junior high athletes have egos of kings
As they lose their capacity to care…

By high school, it's all about being the best
in grades, activities, identity, sex,
and experimentation and 'whatever' comes next,
With no thought for capacity to care…

Thru college and worklife, the picture's the same
Pleasure However, without burden or blame.
Reality's just about winning the game,
Not about a capacity to care…

Jaded in comfort, we've grown to expect
conditioned air, cellphones, internet,
and travel at leisure around the planet
Without need of capacity to care...

While our world is a complex confusing place
with overpopulation, starvation, wars & waste,
very Survival at issue; what a disgrace
That most have no capacity to care...

If each took a moment, each now and again, to consider one thing
beyond self-indulgence, gave even a moment to help mankind
make Sense,
We'd expand our capacity to care,
We'd perhaps be willing to share,
And improve life beyond compare.

New Battle. Same War.

Another day gone. Another week passed.
Some battles were won; Others lost pretty fast.
It's become quite routine, I've lost track of the score.
Every day a new battle—but it's still the same war

You fight for your space, your pride and your turn.
Here or there win a race, but eventually learn
that it takes all your strength just to stay in the saddle.
It's the same lousy war--- just each day a new battle.

If you figure it out, about not living to work,
you can laugh at humanity without being a jerk.
But the fact still remains: There's no point. What's it for?
A new day, a new battle--- and its still the same war.

You can start new each day with a smile on your face,
but it gets pretty tedious when you can't get a break.
Better to accept reality and just try not to rattle.
The war's always in progress--- so be ready for battle.

A big breath, some focus, then off to the front.
Do some quick hocus pocus, then be ready to punt.
The routine is ongoing, to hell with the score.
Just get thru each day's battle, and maybe survive the war.

Shooting Yourself In The Foot?

As if life wasn't tough enough and usually pretty stressed,
days hardly full of fun or play-- rather mostly trials and tests--
do you, too often, follow a mindless compulsion to put
actions first, forget to think, and shoot yourself in the foot?

It's not as if you haven't learned that consequences stem
from reactive, impulsive actions which evolve without a plan;
and, yet, you'll wince then simply shrug as new turmoil takes root.
Does it bother you that, so often, you've shot yourself in the foot?

Isn't it a shame and waste of precious perishable time
to, so often, be treading water without logic, reason or rhyme?
Couldn't you, after two backsteps, move forward three--- then look
and think, for just a second, to avoid that shot at the foot?

Just remove the ammo from your gun, the temptation to jump first.
Remember back to childhood, when you had a natural thirst
for scheming before taking a step--- remember the courage it took?
It's so much easier getting thru life not shooting yourself in the foot.

A PEACEFUL MOMENT

Has it really been so long ago since I could always find
a peaceful moment for myself — a quiet, silent time?

It used to be that I could walk along a stretch of beach
with sounds which brought me solace—
rippling waves or whistling breeze.

And whether its a beach walk or a mountain trail I choose,
the offense doesn't go away — the peace still gets abused
by passenger jets and highway whine from people on the move,
most selfishly ignoring the cacophony they choose
to inflict upon the rest of us. Assaulted without consent.
How sad we've lost the wonder of the Peaceful Moment.

I Coulda, Woulda, Shoulda

'I Coulda, Woulda, Shoulda' is so often our lament
when the outcome of anything is to our detriment,
when we grasp that actions, words or body language we sent
failed to convey the message which had been our real intent.

'Coulda, Woulda, Shoulda,' often the story of our lives,
about opportunities missed or failed to recognize,
by listening just more carefully with pause to analyze
before too quick response, without attempt to empathize.

If only we'd had patience and kept an open mind.
If only we'd been willing to think – just one short pause behind –
to clarify the picture and allow ourselves to find
a better resolution to what's best for all combined.

Perhaps a simple compromise for just what Coulda been,
if we only Woulda practiced some self-discipline.
We Shoulda known much better. But, to our great chagrin,
we'll most likely repeat our process again, and then again.

First Impressions

First impressions are often wrong.
We reach quick decisions and then move on,
believing our instinct is all it's about,
with no reason to give any benefit of doubt.

It could be one's eyes or their smile or frown,
a nervous twitch, or hair greased down,
a weak handshake, a manicure chipped,
a voice too squeaky or speech too clipped.

But often reality is that too quick a reaction,
with decision made on rapid perception,
turns out to have been a short-sighted mistake,
with opportunity passed and then too late

for a second look, a closer view
to recognize deeper attributes,
Tempering temptation to hastily decide
whether another few minutes are justified
to look a bit deeper, and avoid the cost
of a wrong first impression and opportunity lost.

What We Can And Can't Control!

The world around us happens without consideration,
for who we are, or how we feel, or our interpretation.
Our inner-voices, dreams or cares are irrelevant to impact;
we can't control what happens – only how we choose to react.
With anger, fear, frustration, dismay, confusion, awe;
to accept, reject, ignore, reflect, act strongly or withdraw.
There's always some reaction to something that occurred --
what we may have witnessed, may have dreamed, or simply heard.
Most reactions are instinctive. To pause and think first is tough,
about whether or whatever is happening truly matters enough
to override our common sense about the next impact
from failing to control how we choose to react.
How we could or should instead have done that or said this?
How we might have reacted somewhat calmer than we did?
How all that followed afterwards – wasted energy, stress, frustration –
were pointless in the scheme of things, just useless aggravation.
So, if and when, we'd take a breath to gather our perspective,
before reacting emotionally with anger or invective,
the likelihood for Common Sense to guide what follows later,
and likelihood for Best Outcome is certainly much greater.

Part III

The Wonders, The Bummers

Midwest Values

There's a place called Middle America, a couple thousand miles away,
Amidst hogs and cows and cornfields under skies perpetually gray,
Where the biggest battles most days are heat, humidity and stench,
With cyclones, ice storms or freezing cold battling the few days left.
Mosquitoes big as golf balls, and just as hard to swat.
Fashion changes every other decade, and a stop sign means you stop.

So many negative images are conjured in my mind,
They usually overshadow other recollections of that time.
Yet back 2000 miles ago in the boring, flat Midwest,
'Growing up' not really that bad, certainly much less stressed.
Life seemed so much simpler then, what was, and how things went,
Although, most likely, it was just my naiveté coupled with innocence.

No seatbelt laws or airbag flaws or helmets for my bike.
We hitch-hiked rides to anywhere, at any time of night.
We played outdoors with balls and sticks, or wrestled out of breath.
We learned about the other sex without fear of transmitted death.
Busted often for lots of pranks, but seldom causing harm,
Grownups accepted our rites-of-passage without undue alarm.

Living by the golden rule was, then, a simple deal.
We learned that folks remember the way you make them feel.
And tried our best to remember a simple reality:
The more sure you are of anything, the more wrong you can be.
As much as I complained back then, couldn't wait to move away,
I realize now how Midwest values impact my life today.

The Space Between His Thoughts

Anxious, lest his time be gone before the final stanza of his song,
though his mind's eye senses this is wrong
In the space between his thoughts.

Fearful that he'll fail to meet commitments made without entreat,
while silent signs point down a different street
In the space between his thoughts.

Rushing to judgment with perception so callous
is the height of his arrogance, despite lack of malice,
while the cosmic message still screams for solace
In the space between his thoughts.

Speed up. Get done. His senses urge.
Back up, Slow down. He senses the word
which patiently waits to ultimately be heard
In the space between his thoughts.

Sometime life slaps him silly. Sometimes he gets a hug.
Sometimes he feels like the windshield.
Sometimes he knows he's the bug.

In My Dreams Tonite

The Power Of Your Aura
Pervades My Quietude,
I'll See You In My Dreams Tonite
To Share This Marvelous Mood.

Reflecting On My Image
Of Perfection Which Surrounds You,
A Dreamscape Is A Perfect Place
To Appreciate That I Found You.

Warmed By Rays Of Sundown,
Envisioning Your Glistening Smile,
Soothed By The Tease Of Evening's Breeze,
I'll See You In Awhile.

The Neverending Airflight Line

Air flights are quite miraculous, in the sense of what transpires—
bodies moved from here to there in a tube with wings and tires.

Most flights are comfortable enough, even reasonably on time;
the disconcerting problem is The NeverEnding Line.

It begins with Line of traffic just to reach the terminal door.
Then comes the Line for ticket checks – so slow moving, such a bore.

If you choose to check your luggage, besides patience and a prayer,
that Line requires endurance - it's a long while you'll be there.

The Security Line is slower still, with bleeps and beeps you hate,
until a lengthy corridor march in Line to reach your gate.

Gate Line to retrieve a boarding pass, then Line to board the plane,
another Line to find your seat, and hopefully storage space.

The takeoff Line of planes and planes is impressive from afar,
but sitting in Line without airflow, stuffier than a bar.

Eventually descending in the 'holding pattern' Line,
you land and stand, and wait and wait while passengers unwind.

Hurry up to wait in Line praying baggage will show up,
then yet another Line to check the tags. Enough's enough!

Air flights are quite miraculous: you were there and now you're here.
The NeverEnding Line is just the price you pay, it's clear.

About Traffic

New York traffic – an experience which
is hardly describable in any language.
Congestion, cacophony, every move on the run,
breathtaking adventure – all rolled into one!
Five boroughs of chaos, ten taxis per head,
except if it's raining or (heaven forbid)
when you're late for an airplane or meeting a date.
New York traffic – an experience to hate.

Italian traffic – now there's an event!
"Your life in your hands" is the message that's sent.
It's three-way or five-way or no way at all.
The freeways are raceways (just minus the call').
Like noisome mosquitoes, the stinky small cars
zip in and zip out from wherever you are.
With their horns and their fingers, Rome drivers express
their frustration with life – a ridiculous mess.

Los Angeles traffic – a sight to behold –
All lined up and waiting with no place to go.
No tollways or bridges, very few radar traps,
using gallons and gallons and gallons of gas.
With eight lanes to navigate, tension often runs high,
but at least there's a view of mountains and sky
with crisp, clean beaches, and seldom too hot.
Compared with the others, LA's best of the lot.

Crazy Downhill Skiers

To one who's not a skier, evaluating from afar,
a skier's fascination is, at best, a bit bizarre.
It's tough to comprehend the joy of aches and stress and strain
just to get atop a mountain, then risk life and limb. Insane?
Nor is it easily comprehensible to a warm-blooded logical soul,
the 'joy' from obvious discomfort of chilling, freezing cold.

It's shivering just to imagine what 'minus degrees' would mean.
How dizzying heights and piercing winds with danger, often extreme,
would captivate, exhilarate, and provide 'ultimate thrill'
to anyone with sanity. Then, after that, there's still
hassle with travel, lodging and clothing,
the shlepping of equipment, with dependency on snow.

Always fear of rocks & treetops, icy patches, crust or glaze,
fog or sleet and glaring sun turning quick to shadow or haze.
Hundreds of dollars in daily fees to ride a ski lift chair
above most certain deathly drops - but surely nothing to fear?
Then finally comes the jump away to shush between the trees,
praying to get down in one piece without tearing ankles or knees.

"So, what's the point?' it's often asked by common non-skier folk.
    What makes the skiers act this way? Is this some crazy joke?
"No way!" say they, the downhillers who've tried it more than once;
    who've experienced the splendor at thousands of feet above.
Where air is pure, pine trees soar, carpet sparkles and glistens,
    where serenity is only surpassed by the soft sound of God whistlin'.

Downhilling is exhilarating and tension evaporates into clouds,
    in the awe-inspiring beauty of the world above the crowds.
A sport for kids as young as three
    or geezers over seventy.
For presidents and kings & queens,
    or simple folk in denim jeans.
With just a modicum of skill,
    anyone can share the skiing thrill.
Most skiers claim, without regrets,
    Downhill Skiing is good as it gets!

But the greatest pleasure, and often tough,
    is the joy of getting those ski boots off!!

A Western Ranch Is A Slice Of Heaven

You don't have to be a cowboy
to enjoy a western horse
or find peace on open range;

You don't have to be a cowgirl
to lope a mountain course
or enjoy campfire flame;

A ranch is for the folk who
simply love the fresh outdoors
and appreciate a change.

A western ranch is a slice of heaven.

Whether fisherman or hiker
looking for quiet retreat
a ranch is perfect-plus;

Whether grownup or little piker,
families young or near complete
mix the splendor with trail dust;

Clearly not a place for dieters,
    ranch food's meat, taters & bread,
        with desserts always a must.

A western ranch is a slice of heaven.

Whether trail walking beginners
    or smoothly loping experts,
        horseback riders are unique;

Balanced smoothly in their saddles,
    guiding gently with their reins,
        smiling thru chill, wind, rain or heat;

Sitting high in western stirrups,
    gliding through wildflower plains,
        riding horses can't be beat.

A western ranch is a slice of heaven.

Usually miles from civilization,
    isolated and self-sufficient,
        each is truly one-of-a-kind;

Inconvenient by intention,
    but so secure and private,
        the ranch guests never mind;

You don't have to be a cowpoke
    to appreciate the pleasure
        of nature's wonders so combined.

A western ranch is a slice of heaven.

Age 8

Full of boundless energy,
always skipping joyfully
as fantasies unfold.
What would you pay to relive one day
as an innocent 8 year old?

Walk plop in any puddle,
step smack in doggie duddle,
but never on a crack.
Would you grab the chance to hop, skip, dance
to an 8 year old playback?

Play on concrete, mud or sand.
one-minute flat attention span—
except for TV time.
You'd know no fear, with grown-ups near,
but on principle, you'd whine.

Soccer, swim or basketball,
roller skate or climb a wall,
cowboy hat and gun.
Only arithmetic makes you sick.
8 year olds have only fun.

PART I

THE MEANING OF LIFE

Macaroni, jellyroll.
    Cheerios without a bowl.
        No need for fork or knife.
Personality for all to see.
    8 year olds live quite a life.

Wicked and mischievous grin,
    slightly cheating to help you win—
        that's how the game was played.
Can't you just see how neat it would be
    to be 8 for just one day?

Proud as you could ever be.
    Unbounded love from family.
        How 'bout a one day trade?
They're right; youth's wasted on the young,
    and 8 year olds have it made!

DEAR GRANDSON ALMOST

To Baby in formation - my grandson almost:
Your mother, my daughter, your magnificent host
who joyously anticipates your coming arrival,
suggested this message for your adulthood archival.

Eighteen years from today, I wonder what might
be of interest to you (and yet doesn't sound trite)
about the world and family who await this event,
with anxious exuberance (and slight torment)?

It's a strange world we live in, in 2003.
On one end of the spectrum is our technology
expanding at a pace so rapid and extreme,
that most of us can't comprehend - even dream--

what this world will look like even five years away.
Yes, it's a strange strange world we live in today.
On the other side are billions of people who live
by 'survival instinct', taking more than they give.

Pursuing the spoils of material stuff–
their basic perspective: thinking 'never enough.'
So "taking" and "fighting" are still daily events;
after thousands of years, humans still don't get it.

Gangs, crime, wars, revenge, hate and malice
all compete to keep the world way out of balance.
Hopefully by the time you're reading this letter,
we won't have blown ourselves up and things will be better.

So much of the problem is simple selfishness and greed,
'survival of the fittest' has long been the human creed.
But some families are different, especially our clan–
we care and we share as much as we can.

The family you're entering is loving and close;
we treat each other with respect and try harder than most
to share time, thoughts and friendship, as well as our stuff;
to appreciate what we have and acknowledge our love.

So as you read this and look back, I mostly hope you will see
that the person you've become was shaped by these things.
That as much as your classroom and learnings have taught,
our family traditions have influenced your thought;

that you carry those traditions into your adult years,
that your integrity and wisdom overcome anger or fears,
that you honor your family—and especially your mother—
who awaits your arrival with unconditional love,

and that you'll always remember, whatever the menace,
you can always depend on your loving Poppa Dennis.

PART IV

END OF AN ERA

Ours Is A Strange Society...

Have you ever noticed that, whenever pause allows
    you time to focus briefly on the whens and whys and hows,

you notice minor changes in your program or grand plan
    are all it takes to screw things up and turn intention to sand?

What is the bigger problem, often it is pondered:
    Ignorance, Apathy, or just opportunity squandered?

'I don't know and I don't care' - the typical response.
    We may not know the answers but we know our needs and wants.

Ours is a strange society where conflicts much abound
    between all types of people fighting for their ground,

whether religion, age or race, politics or sport,
    environment, animal rights, beliefs of every sort,

irrespective of positions or arguments that matter,
    our species' selfish nature is a constant equalizer.

As are ticket lines, security checks, bathrooms at events,
    traffic lights, parking lots - usually, it makes no sense:

government office or food counter with only one line open,
    while people spend their lives in lines, with barely a word spoken.

All waiting, watching, irritated - most staring into space
    as time, energy and focus all dissipate to waste.

Ours is a strange society: plodding forward as we're allowed,
    while selfishly and fanatically just trying to hold our ground.

Bye-Bye Liberty?

It's Election Night late, 2008, in the former land of the free.
America turned a page today which could lock out liberty.
The masses, who are asses, got it ass backwards for sure,
and cast their votes against the past instead of for the future.

Angered, rightfully, at perceived ineptitude and greed
of Mr. Bush's cronies, along with his arrogant creed,
voters opted to move the pendulum far toward the other end.
Many shrugged "what could be worse?" but failed to comprehend

that beyond a bungled foreign war and recession economy,
disdain from other nations, or the rights of state autonomy,
is the real Threat to our society, indeed Western Civilization,
from fanatical extremists bent on global capitulation

to convoluted orders channeled through a prophet's breath,
demanding absolute obedience, under penalty of death,
for return to an ancient culture with no conception of 'freedom'
(but for self-appointed clergy ruling through trepidation).

Now that America has anointed a radical left position
    which espouses cooperation with extremists and socialism,
who plan to submit our future to the vote of world approval,
    'Liberty' is eventually headed towards pink slip removal.

Once ago, Americans had freedom to think as wished,
    to speak without concern about offending 'sensitiveness.'
`to fuel their minds and bodies with what anyone suggested,
    to work with whom they chose, unconstrained by 'political correctness.'

Freedom began to dissipate when personal frustrations
    of flower-powered adolescents with naive imaginations
regulated communications just so others wouldn't "feel bad"—
    limiting what can be said and to whom. How incredibly sad!

Soon left-wing liberals and extremists will push for full control
    over behaviors of the rest of us (their fundamental goal),
and more absolute and rigid rules will become priority—
    eventually resulting in the lock out of liberty.

Diminishing America

It's the early days of 2019 and America's structure is coming apart,
So many voices, so many fronts, off to a very rough start.
Any governance 'on behalf of the people' a joke in every way,
While politicians vie for power, motivated by personal greed and hate.
The shameful behavior of Congress and bias of media publications
Are absurd, self-serving, insulting to citizens and the Nation.

Federal government, local school closures, southern border disputes,
'Harassment' complaints commonplace, guilt by allegation versus proof.
A mantra of undefined 'Political Correctness' now pre-empts all else,
Ignoring what's best for country-at-large, just what "feels" best for oneself.
Acceptance of power-at-any-cost justified by pursuit of ideology,
With fake and phony messaging to mask overwhelming hypocrisy.

Captive media and 'Talking Heads' have abandoned all pretense
Of true or balanced reporting, in pursuit of growing audience,
With rampant, arrogant, personal bias overriding any degree
Of responsibly informing their audience, ignoring responsibility.
Focus instead on hourly 'Alerts' with continuous warning of peril
In every facet of modern life, but with 'facts' contradictory and sterile.

Beyond absurdity of media control, hypocritically blaring away,
Manipulating so many to believe just what they heard that day,
'Decisions' from unaccountable 'judges' based on personal bias,
A court system moving at snail pace, the country drowning in chaos.
A battle for power and money, fueled by capitalism's creed,
diminished respect for democracy with no moral position to lead.

One Party's priorities are essentially Security, Principles and Precedent;
The other focusing on Voters, and Personality of the President.
Blind to the schism which animosity creates, manipulation to 'take sides,'
Most confused, divided and angry, precluded from compromise.
It's the early days of 2019 as civilized structure is coming apart,
So many voices, so many fronts, and off to a very rough start.

A Shame It Couldn't Last

Financial times for the wealthy-enough were mostly pretty great
until the global economy badly crashed in 2008.

Most had become accustomed, at simple beck and call,
to Objects of Desire - opportunity to 'have it all'.

Ensconced in Material Comfort and pursuit of constant Pleasure,
with objective just to maximize, in no uncertain measure,

the toys, tools and time to fully appreciate life,
unaware the world would soon transform to total strife.

Their opportunity to have lived in midst of recent decades past,
was certainly 'A Good Run' - what a shame it couldn't last.

But greed and avarice won out; 'haves' thought they didn't have enough,
and watched Houses of Cards topple rather than share their stuff.

From then on, some fortunes would go up, others upside down,
the Future mortgaged for trillions when grandkids are around

to deal with aftermath from this mess – the crisis that they caused.
A Shame the Good Times Couldn't Last; a shame so much was lost.

The Coronavirus Crisis

It's now mid-2020, the entire world on edge.
Just a temporary pandemic, as all Experts still pledge.
Virus just a form of flu which for centuries has attacked,
with our species so far always successful fighting back.

This one quite more serious, having taken a course
which ignored territorial boundaries with contagion force,
Infecting people silently, transmitting quickly with ease,
but experts diagnosing as a manageable disease,

With relatively simple steps to mitigate its impact:
avoiding large gatherings and cautious personal contact,
Not breathing air or touching others' skin or things they've touched—
plastic/metal/fabric (everything pretty much).

This medical crisis genuine and serious to be sure,
exacerbated by 24/7 barrage of "Pandemic! Still no cure!"
By the media mob fighting to keep audience tuned-in,
with always scary headlines and half-truth opinion,

From 'expert' talking-heads and selfish politicians,
    extolling propaganda for election-slant positions.
With Smartphones screaming 'Crisis' in a manner so frantic,
    that so many have been driven to levels of Panic,

Who then overwhelmed resources, raided and hoarded supplies,
    feared all outside contact, and failed to realize
That most of their Panic was simply explained—
    a result of overanxious, self-inflicted pain.

Like crises before, Covid-19 too shall pass
    and the world will reset, although alas,
Like outcomes before, those Fittest Survive—
    those who focus on sensible priorities and strive

To act responsibly and to do what's 'right,'
    maintaining positive outlook for a future still bright.
So try to stay positive, don't succumb to fright;
    just relax, keep socially distanced, and sit tight.

Implosion Of Society

Witnessing implosion of society, no one with eyes & ears could help
but feel dismayed by evidence of our culture's path toward hell.
Gone are respect for private thoughts, discussions, choice,
The manner of raising children (confused whether girls or boys).

Kids who once accepted guidance about evolution, purpose, religion,
not radical ideologies about stuff like 'equity' or 'transition.'
We're headed towards a society that few yet imagine, much less desire,
'rules' dictated by whomever-in-power with obedience required.

Now autocratic decision process facilitates abusive corruption,
while those failing to cooperate are deemed guilty of disruption.
Across the planet, every hundred years or so, societies reset
their culture and expectations, when great-grandchildren feel no debt

to preceding generations, who toiled and even died,
enabling and protecting our social system to survive.
But *what it is, is what it is*, and we're about to learn
that this generation's path is past the point of no return.

Past The Point Of No Return

Once upon a quieter time, looking backward from today,
our world seemed pretty stable in most important ways.
Folks woke up most mornings with 'great new day' perception,
and little wasted energy on the last bizarre election.
Just a few decades later, the picture greatly changed
as Progressivism fomented a country much deranged.
24/7 news always clamoring about
dangerous 'Identity Groups,' creating anxiety and doubt,
with urgent hourly issues always critical to our lives,
but most unable or willing to simply recognize
that Talking Heads and biased 'news' do not reflect Reality,
and often fail to reflect even simplest shreds of sanity.

While propaganda diverts us from issues that really matter,
culture fast evaporates, the American Dream gets shattered.
Power struggles, gender politics, demands for Reparation,
while social media applauds nuclear family separation,
Religious wars still raging after many thousand years,
while media and politicians still play to peoples' fears.
Democracy in tatters, capitalism on the run,
felons mass-released from prisons, some allowed to carry guns.
Government regulations increasing every year,
as censorship increases and freedoms disappear.

The Dream's become a figment of generations past,
    'Retirement' for too many now a dream with little chance.

It's safe to say that most were shocked by recent election results,
    which have clearly demonstrated the Nation's changing pulse.
For sure, too late to wrestle back that once-upon-a-time
    when Stability was a good thing, when Security felt just fine,
when elected leaders were trusted to serve the common good,
    and workers simply did their best to provide as best they could.
Being American is a privilege that way too few respect,
    now watching their dreams drift away, due mostly to neglect.
Stupidly and shamefully, now too late to turn around
    a disappearing culture, from behavior run aground
by Progressive Activists with mass media support,
    attacking any differing views, promoting 'socialism' for sport.

Fueled by Activists and billionaires pursuing power/ money/ fame,
    as widening partisanship keeps Others always at blame,
perceiving most opposed perspective as purely 'anti-me,'
    unwilling to even listen to positions contradictory,
with 'feelings' emanating from fake or biased news,
    while Confirmation Bias negates all opposing views.
We see implosion everywhere at an ever-increasing pace,
    on a path to where democracy could find itself erased.
One by one, structures crumble – authority, politics, religion,
    respect for others' cultures, family values or tradition –
with priorities mostly focused on personal 'rights' and 'feel,'
    not country or community but rather 'What's In It For Me!'

Anger and antagonism keep increasing at a pace
    which tears the country wide apart. What a tragic waste!
From all appearance, at this point, from all we've failed to learn,
    we're truly heading rapidly toward massive crash & burn,
        with America sadly heading past the Point of No Return

The Edge Of Wisdom

Some say we're getting pretty close to a point where we will find
some answers to the purpose of the universe grand design.

Others think that's ludicrous and contend we're nowhere near
any vector of the time/space point, to maybe make it clear

that alter ego, edged aside, our species is little more
than a minor note in a symphony by some higher-power scored.

As thought by all the wisest minds just a few generations ago,
our world was flat and center stage for the Stars and Planets Show,

performed twice-daily every day for amusement and desires
of our master-species human race. (No deeper thought required.)

As science and discoveries have taught some truths and facts,
True, humans have shown tenacity, which other species lacked.

Yet, for all the knowledge we accumulate from zillions of data bits,
little evidence shows of "wisdom" which could have grown from this.

In the scheme of things our species has, for all that it's been through,
    less relevance than a speck of sand to the planetary hue.

So the questions still remain: What are we doing here?
    Where do we go? Why don't we learn from our giant ecosphere?

One puzzling observation is: It's simple, but complex,
    with multi-level "balance"—so fragile in most respects.

And my thought makes it simpler still: that balance needs priority.
    Like spokes of a wheel tethered to framework of reality,

Each of life's acts must blend and dance, synchronizing with a script.
    Unless each act follows the plan, life become a pilotless ship

Which bobs and treads through endless seas without a destination;
    We need to set priorities as a mainstay for civilization.

As long as we, the human race, put off setting a "priority system,"
    it's ridiculous to imagine that we'd reach the edge of wisdom.

PART V

THOUGHTS CAPTURED IN SCULPTURE

Pondering

Illusion Of Control

Now What

Turmoil

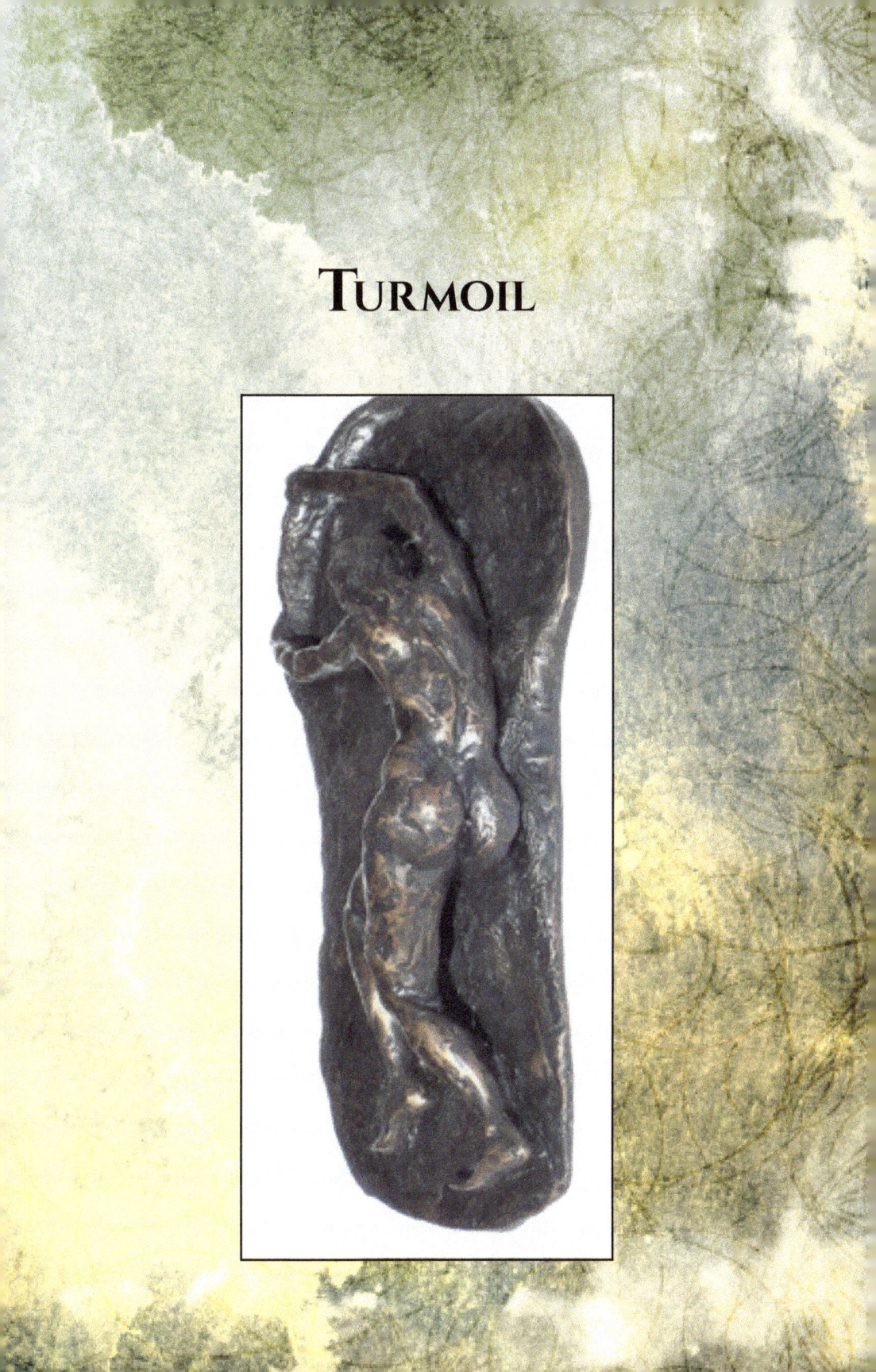

MYSTERY

Before & After

Sexuality At Rest

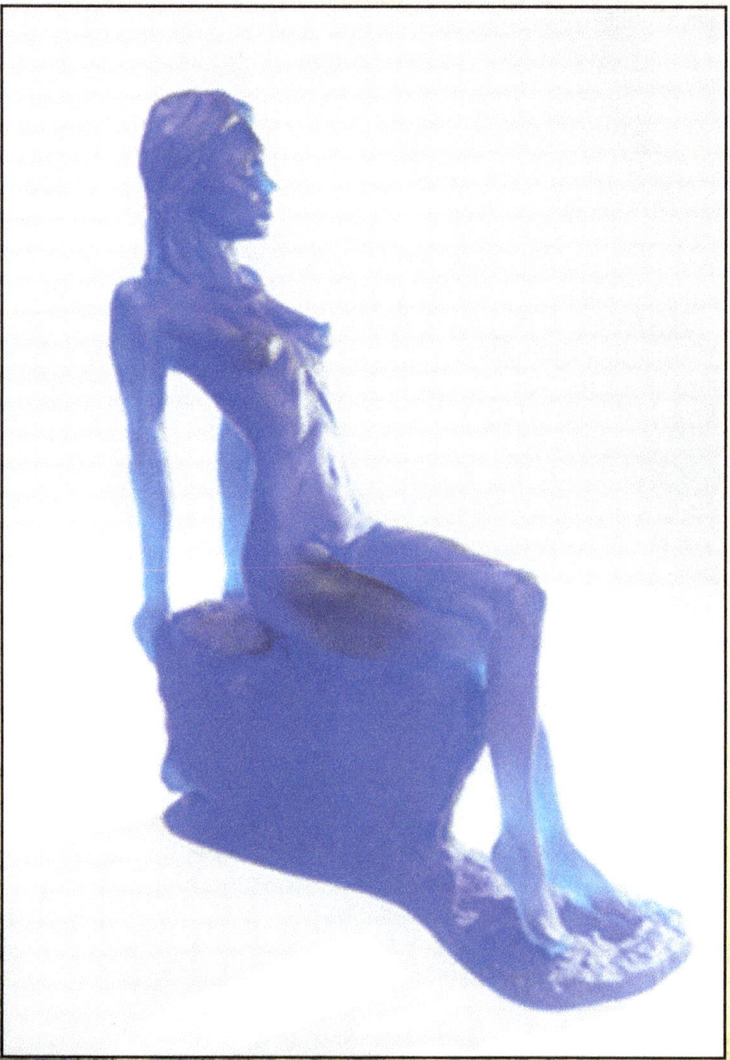

Lazy Daze

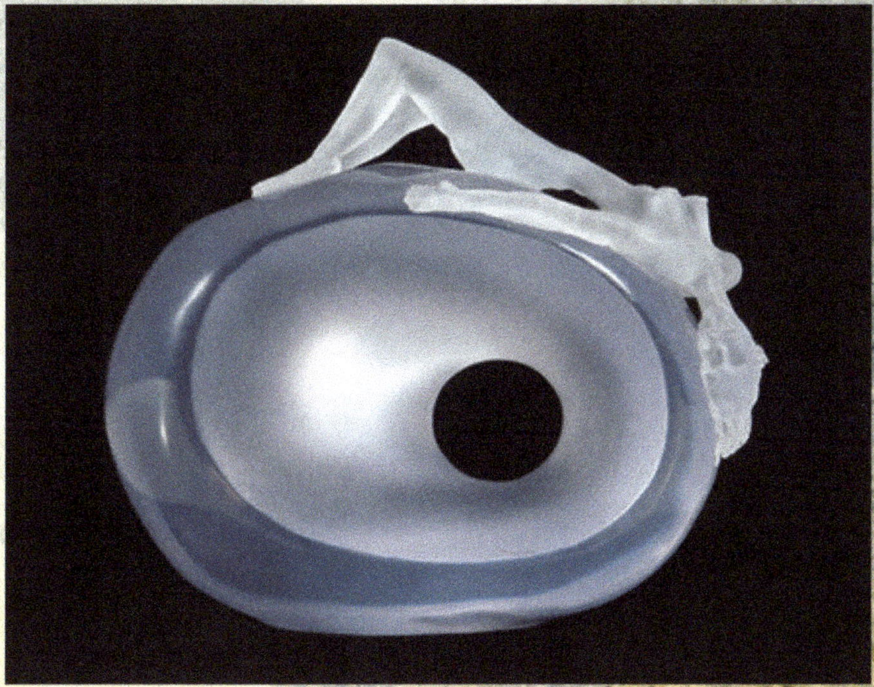

Romanesque

Wood Nymph

Forest Nymphs

Ancestor

Mousetrap

Dreamband

ANGEL

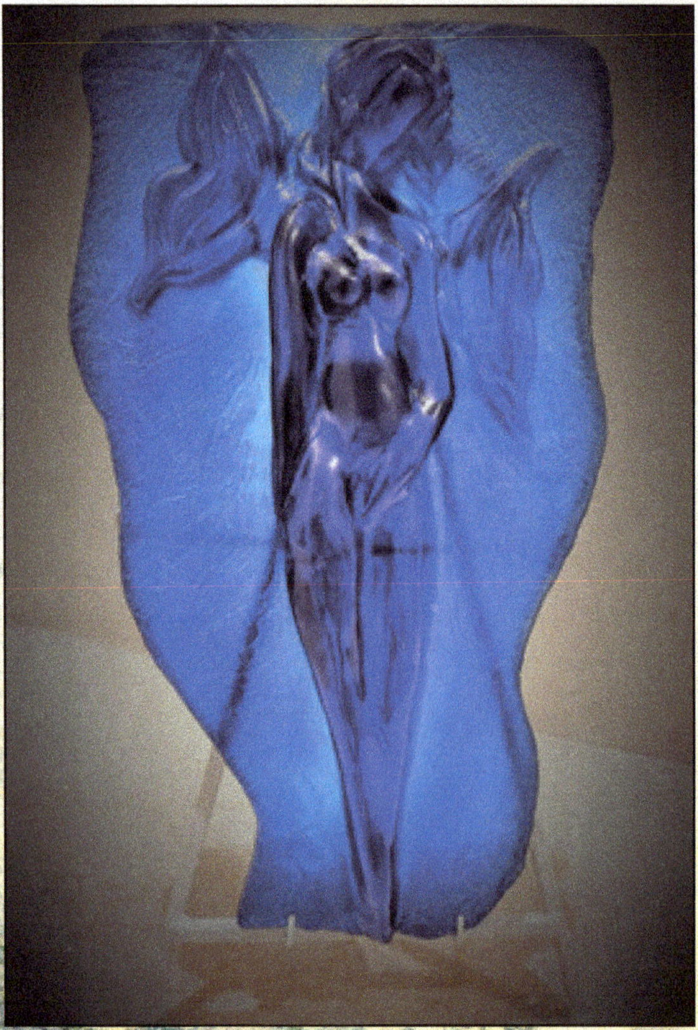

Printed in the USA
CPSIA information can be obtained
at www.ICGtesting.com
LVHW062354170224
772035LV00020B/309

9 781960 758033